Sedona

TREASURE *of the* SOUTHWEST

by KATHLEEN BRYANT

NORTHLAND PUBLISHING

Contents

Natural History 7

Cultural History 23

Contemporary Sedona 39

Nearby Attractions 57

Sedona was founded in 1902 and incorporated in 1988. The greater Sedona area, including Oak Creek Canyon and the Village of Oak Creek, is home to about fifteen thousand residents. At an elevation of 4,500 feet, Sedona has a mild four-season climate, though one could easily make the argument for five seasons, including a dry foresummer and the monsoon. Annual rainfall averages 17 inches, with August the wettest month at about 2 ¹/₂ inches. Although temperature extremes range from 0 to 108F°, average daily temperatures fall between 46 and 75F°.

Introduction

S EDONA. . . THE VERY NAME SOUNDS SIBILANT, inviting, even a bit mysterious. Some point out it's an anagram for "anodes" and an indication that powerful earth energies emanate from red rock canyons and spires. No less significant is that Sedona is actually the name of a woman, one of the first to carve out a life in an isolated, rough land, where life was balanced by breathtaking beauty and hard work.

Red Rock Country is a place of intensely blue skies, greens of every hue, and reds and golds from the palest peach to the deepest vermilion. It's also an in-between place, not as vast as the Grand Canyon, three hours to the north, nor as extreme as the Sonoran Desert, little more than an hour to the south. Here, the scenic vistas are closer, friendlier, inviting exploration.

Sparkling Oak Creek draws humans and wildlife alike to its lush banks. Seasons add variety, with springtime wildflowers, summer thunderstorms, fall colors, and wintery snow and fog. The mild climate makes it possible to enjoy the natural setting all year long.

Sedona is a place of contrasts and even contradictions. Ephemeral waterfalls cascade down sheer rock walls after a rain, sometimes lasting only an hour before vanishing. Delicate wildflowers burst from dry, rocky soil. Small town charm elbows up beside artistic sophistication. Here, it's possible to sweat your way deep into a craggy canyon and watch sunset paint the cliffs impossible colors, and then sit down to dinner at an elegant restaurant later that evening.

New Age pilgrims, big-city refugees, outdoor enthusiasts, retirees, artists, and cowboys make up a diverse, even quirky, community. Red rock fever—the longing to connect with this incredible place—is easy to catch, hard to cure, and in advanced cases, accompanied by a fierce sense of responsibility to the land.

Those who take the time to explore will connect with Sedona's Red Rock Country at even deeper levels. Heart-stealing vistas wait at nearly every turn in the road or trail. But intimate moments—hearing a hawk's cry echo from canyon walls or feeling a link to the people who took shelter in sandstone alcoves centuries ago—come with patience and an open heart.

This book is a tour in words and pictures, beginning with the age-old forces that created Sedona's red rock landscape, and then introducing the people, plants, and animals that call it home. It also introduces a few of the many ways to experience Sedona, as well as nearby communities and attractions, where nature, history, art, and adventure await. May your journey be magical.

A Guide to the Rock Formations

*View from Airport Mesa

The top of Airport Mesa, five hundred feet above West Sedona, offers commanding views to the north and west. Work on the airport began in the early 1950s. Boys from the Christian Indian School and a local scout troop helped clear rocks from the runway. By 1958, the airport had a thirty-seven hundred feet long clay airstrip and four permanently based aircraft…but no gas. When pilots needed to refuel, they flew in circles above town to signal Joe Moser, who owned a service station in Uptown. When he spotted a circling plane, Moser headed for the mesa with fuel. Today, the mesa is the site of several commercial air tour companies, a terminal building, restaurant, and motel.

1. Doe Mesa—A mile-long trail up this steep-sided mesa leads to sweeping views of Red Rock Country and the Verde Valley. The trailhead for this hike and the Bear Mountain trail is on Boynton Pass Road, a rugged unpaved road through what was once cattle country.

2. Bear Mountain—Are there bears on this mountain? Probably not, since black bears prefer canyon woodlands and forests. It is said the 6,541-foot peak got its name because it appears bear-shaped from above. A 3-mile trail leads to the top, from which hikers can spot Flagstaff's San Francisco Peaks. This trail is strenuous and exposed—definitely not for novices.

3. Chimney Rock—The inspiration for this rock's name is obvious, at least from this perspective. People who live along Dry Creek Road and view it from the west refer to it as Three-Finger Rock.

4. Lizard Head—This sentinel reptile watches over West Sedona and the backcountry north of Capitol Butte. Some people say the lizard's body is within the butte, with his tail coming out the other side and forming the natural sandstone arch called Devil's Bridge.

5. Capitol Butte—This dome-shaped mountain has also been known through the decades as Grayback, Saddlerock, and Thunder Mountain.

At 6,355 feet, it is one of the highest peaks in the Sedona area and can disappear into the clouds during a winter storm. People in tune with earth energies and past lives believe it hides a vast crystal chamber or a lost Lemurian city.

Devil's Bridge

6. West Sedona—This part of town, once known as Grasshopper Flats, was relatively unpopulated even as late as the 1960s. Before that time, many movies were filmed in the flats. They are remembered today by street names such as Fabulous Texan Way and Johnny Guitar Circle.

Grasshopper Flats, circa 1955.

11. Posse Grounds—This former rodeo arena, seen in *The Rounders*, became the first city park about the time Sedona was incorporated in 1988. It has picnic ramadas, playground, and ball fields.

12. Wilson Mountain—About eight million years ago, lava flowed over the top of this mountain, the tallest in Sedona at 7,122 feet. The mountain was named after Richard Wilson, an ill-fated bear hunter. One day in 1885, the hunter encountered a grizzly, and this time the bear hunted him. Wilson Canyon, where his body was eventually found, is also named for him.

14. Piñon-Juniper Woodland—The predominant ecological zone in the red rocks is affectionately referred to by foresters as "PJ." It is home to a diverse population of plants, from delicate spring wildflowers to hardy agave and yucca, and animals, including coyotes, rattlesnakes, and javelina. Junipers bear bluish "berries," which are actually modified cones. Piñons have cones that conceal small nuts, a staple for many animals and birds and a traditional food of Southwestern Indian tribes. Though PJ forests are small in stature, they can be great in age. Piñons with a trunk diameter of six to ten inches might be more than a century old.

7. Sugarloaf—In pioneer times, when this butte was named, sugar didn't come in cubes or granules. It came in a lump or cone and was referred to as a sugar loaf. The top of this butte is a good place to "loaf" and watch young ravens at play. This and other open spaces close to the city are on U.S. Forest Service land. The Red Rock Ranger district refers to these urban forest areas as Sedona's "neighborwoods."

8. Coffee Pot Rock—Below this landmark rock formation once stood a Western town, the Coffee Pot movie set. John Wayne had it built in 1945 for his film *Angel and the Badman*. It was used in many other Westerns before being razed to make way for a rapidly expanding population.

9. Soldier's Pass—This break in the cliffs was once a route for soldiers from Fort Verde, who camped here in the 1860s and 70s to fish and hunt. They called the area Camp Garden.

10. Lost Wilson Mountain—This 6,762-foot peak isn't really lost but does appear to be disconnected from the rest of the plateau that forms Wilson Mountain and the west rim of Oak Creek Canyon.

Richard Wilson's gravesite.

13. Ship Rock—This rock formation's triangular "sail" soars over Uptown Sedona. Ship Rock's monumental shape can be spotted from as far away as Jerome.

View from Chapel of the Holy Cross*

Pioneer Abraham James named many local rock formations. He called this area, where the Chapel of the Holy Cross now stands, Little Horse Park. He also named Big Park, where the Village of Oak Creek is today. "Park" referred to the open grasslands that were mixed in with the piñon-juniper woodland. Both areas were grazed by livestock. Little Horse Park was the setting for the Quaker family's homestead in John Wayne's *Angel and the Badman* (1946). Nearly a decade later, it became the site of the Catholic chapel designed by heiress Marguerite Brunswick Staude.

1. Madonna—When Marguerite Brunswick Staude spotted this rock, she considered it confirmation that she had chosen the right site for her Chapel of the Holy Cross, declaring, "As I stood on this pinnacle and looked northeast, there stood the madonna and child, carved by nature into its nearly perfect form."

2. The Nuns—This pair of prominent spires is referred to as The Nuns. Interestingly, many nuns and priests visited the site as the chapel was being built. Construction supervisor Fred Coukos recalled one incident with embarrassment. He had just finished "cussing out" an erring worker and turned to find the entire scene had been witnessed by a priest.

View from Uptown*

Today, bustling Uptown Sedona is home to dozens of shops, galleries, restaurants, and motels. Yet only a few decades ago, Uptown's sleepy small-town scene was dominated by fruit orchards, with businesses geared to local residents, including a service station, post office, grocery store, and bar. The historic architectural style, referred to as "red rock territorial," combines board and batten with local red sandstone. One thing that hasn't changed is the view—Uptown is a great place to sit down with a cup of coffee or an ice cream cone and gaze at the rocks.

6. Giant's Thumb—The tip of the Giant's Thumb, also known as Thumb Butte, marks the end of Mitten Ridge, a scene that dazzles travelers on Schnebly Hill Road.

7. Schnebly Hill—Once upon a time, the road that leads up this chaparral-covered slope was the quickest route for Verde Valley farmers and ranchers to haul produce to Flagstaff or drive cattle up to cooler pastures on the Mogollon Rim.

8. Munds Mountain—This 6,834-foot mountain was named for the Munds family, whose members included William, the mayor of Jerome after it incorporated in 1899; John, a respected Yavapai county sheriff; and Frances, the first woman in Arizona to be elected State Senator.

Munds Mountain Wilderness

3. Gibraltor—The beautiful buff-colored cliffs of Gibraltor mark the edge of the Munds Mountain Wilderness Area, one of three federally designated wildernesses in the region of the red rocks. Together, they total more than 140,000 acres.

4. Courthouse Butte—This graceful formation was originally named Church Rock by Abraham James, whose family settled along Oak Creek in 1879, not far from where today's Kings Ransom Inn stands on Hwy. 179. Thanks to a mapmaker's error, the butte was later labeled Courthouse, a name that James applied to the formation we now know as Cathedral Rock.

5. Bell Rock—Bell Rock is considered to be an "electric" vortex. Its gorgeous slickrock lures people like a magnet, sometimes right out of their rental cars and up its slopes without water or hiking boots, resulting in a high number of rescues and accidents.

---

9. Camel's Head—Because of its bold orange-red and white stripes, some people call this formation Tiger's Head. If you look closely at the ridgeline, you might be able to spot a couple members of the Peanuts gang: Lucy watches as Linus plays the piano.

10. Snoopy—The famous canine is lying on his back in profile, just the way cartoonist Charles Schulz drew him. Snoopy's nose is a block of Fort Apache Limestone, a distinct layer within the common Schnebly Hill formation.

11. Lee Mountain—A man named Lee was the first to settle on Lower Oak Creek near Red Rock Crossing. The mountain named for him stretches south all the way to the Village of Oak Creek.

Snoopy Rock

12. Twin Buttes—It's easy to see how this mirrored pair of buttes got their name. The peak on the right is referred to as The Elephant.

13. Cathedral Rock—From this perspective, the graceful spires and mace of Cathedral Rock look like ancient standing stones. From the other direction, Cathedral Rock is said to be the most photographed scene in Arizona.

Natural History

GEOLOGY

Sedona's colorful buttes, spires, and canyons are carved from the Colorado Plateau, a vast upland extending around the Four Corners area of the Southwest. The southern edge of the plateau, the Mogollon (muggy-own) Rim, forms the escarpments to the north and east of the Sedona area.

Opposite: Munds Mountain's Coconino, Toroweap, and Kaibab layers make a light-colored backdrop for Mitten Ridge.

Above: The snow-topped San Francisco Peaks rise from the Colorado Plateau, with Red Rock Country carved into its southern edge.

Right: Steep-sided Courthouse Butte is a geological layer cake of Schnebly Hill formation topped with Coconino Sandstone.

Pages 8-9: Cockscomb's striking silhouette is comprised of reddish Schnebly Hill formation.

Between the Rim, the Verde Valley to the south, and Sycamore Canyon to the west lies Red Rock Country, approximately five hundred square miles of canyons, grasslands, and colorful sandstone cliffs. The sparkling waters of Oak Creek, fed by springs and snowmelt from the mountains around Flagstaff, flow south through Oak Creek Canyon and the communities of Page Springs and Cornville before joining the Verde River. This magnificent scenery and natural diversity has been in the making for hundreds of millions of years, ages before the first humans took shelter in the sandstone alcoves. It took a succession of ancient seas, deserts, rivers, lava flows, and shifts in the earth's surface to create the colorful buttes and spires of this amazing landscape.

The foundation found in and around Sedona is Redwall limestone, laid down by a shallow tropical sea about 330 million years ago (MYA). Though this layer isn't exposed locally, it plays a key role in providing Sedona's water supply as it houses numerous aquifers. It also forms the occasional sinkhole when underlying limestone dissolves and ceiling layers collapse, such as at Devil's Dining Room. Redwall limestone, which is actually gray in color, is stained red by overlying layers. Incidentally, these layers are red because a thin, oxidized iron deposit coats the individual grains of sand, and iron oxide is, not surprisingly, rusty red.

Overlying the Redwall are four reddish layers known collectively as the Supai group, together about six hundred feet thick, laid down between 320-285 MYA. They formed when the Sedona area was a coastal plain between two seas that rose and fell, leaving alternating sandstone and mudstone. Supai group rocks can be seen in Wilson Canyon beneath Midgely Bridge.

Between 285-275 MYA, a river carried debris from an ancient mountain range near the present-day Rockies, changing course and creating a large floodplain. This led to the Hermit formation, which is slope-forming mudstone, sandstone, and conglomerate. Sedona is built on top of this dark reddish stone. Look for it in road cuts…or underneath your feet.

Next, when you look up, the bright orange-red spires and buttes were coastal sand dunes formed about 275-270 MYA. About seven hundred feet thick, this Schnebly Hill formation appears as subtly shaded horizontal layers. The formation includes four different members or subdivisions. Easily distinguished is the grayish Fort Apache limestone, which on lower formations sometimes forms an erosion-resistant cap rock (such as Snoopy's nose), and elsewhere appears as a ten- to twelve-foot chunky-looking band running through red sandstone.

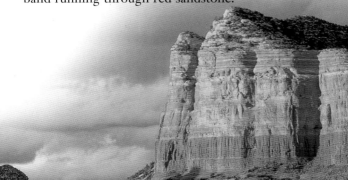

Left: The seven hundred-foot thick Schnebly Hill formation appears as a series of horizontal layers in shades of orange, red, and buff. *Below:* Fort Apache limestone runs through the base of Mitten Ridge and shapes the erosion-resistant carousel of the Merry-Go-Round *(right)* near Schnebly Hill Road.

In the vicinity of Boynton Canyon, the limestone thins out, marking the edge of an ancient sea. After this sea receded, an extensive desert with windblown inland sand dunes covered much of northern Arizona about 270-265 MYA. These dunes created light gold, beautifully cross-bedded Coconino sandstone. Because the dune formation was continuous as the climate changed and coastline shifted, Coconino sandstone merges in places with the reddish Schnebly Hill sandstone, making it difficult to pinpoint exactly where the Coconino layer begins.

Geologists debate how to identify the period from 265-262 MYA, when another shallow sea advanced toward the desert. It formed a three hundred-foot thick layer of sandstone in the Sedona area, but gypsum to the northwest. Whether this layer is termed Coconino sandstone, which it resembles, or called the Toroweap formation, you can see it above a horizontal green band of vegetation on higher peaks.

The overlying Kaibab formation, primarily limestone, was left as the sea expanded about 260-255 MYA. Undersea sponges formed into nodules and beds of chert. The fossil-bearing Kaibab formation shapes the Mogollon Rim, as well as the rim of Grand Canyon.

During these millions of years, continents shifted, creating mountain ranges and rivers that carried away and deposited debris. Lava flows from a volcanic period beginning about 15 MYA formed escarpments and outcroppings. A fault line, the precursor of Oak Creek Canyon, was filled with successive lava flows that were gradually carved out by gravelly run-off.

Geologic forces continue their work, though at a pace we humans rarely consider. The Mogollon Rim continues to recede by one foot every six hundred years. But change can sometimes be quite sudden, as a recent rockfall in Fay Canyon proved when it uprooted trees and buried a hiking trail. Someday, far into the future, this magnificent landscape might be eroded away or covered by another sea. But for now and the foreseeable future, Red Rock Country will continue to inspire both visitors and residents alike.

Of Castles and Kings

Courthouse Butte

Snoopy Rock

Most rock names in Sedona are obvious, although younger folks may be puzzled by a Coffee Pot that doesn't look anything like the automatic drip in their kitchen at home. Obvious shape-named rocks include Steamboat, Ship Rock, Snoopy, Cockscomb, and Teapot Rock. Some, like King Solomon and His Sisters, require a little more imagination.

The less evident the shape, the more likely the name is to be debated. Depending on who you ask, the ridge running east of Snoopy Rock is Camel's Head, Tiger's Head, or Cochise. A hot debate, even today, surrounds two rock names bestowed in the 1870s by pioneer Abraham James (who also named Bell Rock). He identified Church Rock and Court Rock in 1878. Later, a mapmaker switched the two, and they are now known (well, to lots of people, anyway) as Courthouse Rock and Cathedral Rock.

There's no doubt this fantasy red landscape fires the imagination. One so moved was Walt Disney, who named Submarine Rock. Some people believe that the Sedona area inspired the animation in his original *Fantasia*.

FLORA & FAUNA

RED ROCK COUNTRY IS LOCATED within a transition zone between the high Colorado Plateau and the basin-and-range country to the south. At four to six thousand feet in elevation, the climate is moderate, but varies from creekside to canyon to slope depending on orientation of the sun and rainfall amounts. Differences in terrain, soil, and elevation mean different types of habitats for plants and animals.

In desert grasslands west and south of the city, spiky soaptree yucca, saltbush, grama grass, and desert plants such as ocotillo and prickly pear cactus provide food and shelter for lizards, snakes, and roadrunners.

On south-facing slopes, manzanita, mountain mahogany, scrub oak, and other low-growing shrubs form a dense chaparral of green that looks friendly from afar but can be virtually impossible to penetrate for any hiker wandering off trail.

The oak woodlands of dry canyons might include a half-dozen or more species of oak, most of them evergreen, bearing holly-shaped leaves. Some varieties interbreed, and carrying a field guide can be an exercise in futility. Their acorns are a staple for birds and squirrels and were also a traditional food of the Yavapai, who knew how to remove the bitter tannins.

As canyons climb toward the rim, the woodland turns to forest, with ponderosa pine, fir, and spruce. Our mixed conifer forests shelter deer, elk, black bears, Abert's squirrels, and numerous species of birds, including the rare northern goshawk.

Along Oak Creek and West Fork, lush riparian growth supports a number of animals not usually seen in other areas of Red Rock Country, such as ringtails, great blue herons, and tiger salamanders. Crown-shaped golden columbine, canyon grape, New Mexico raspberry, and watercress are a delight—the profuse poison ivy is not.

In canyon washes, hikers will often encounter thick stands of Arizona cypress trees, a holdout population from a cooler, moister climate of centuries past. These beautiful trees have textured and twisted trunks in gorgeous shades of orange, green, and gray, with cool gray-green scale-like leaves.

The most predominant natural community in the red rock area is the piñon-juniper woodland, nicknamed "PJ." Its small trees include one-seed juniper, Utah juniper, and piñon. Of course, plants and animals aren't aware of the neat scientific boundaries assigned to them. Prickly-pear cactus, oak, and rattlesnakes are commonly seen in PJ woodlands that border desert grasslands. This intermixture of species from neighboring communities is referred to as an ecotone, and the area's ecotones offer wondrous variety—over 500 types of plants; 55 mammals; 180 birds; some 35 snakes, lizards, and amphibians; 20 or more varieties of fish; and thousands of insects and invertebrates.

Left: **Four o'clocks bloom in an ecotone of desert grassland and piñon-juniper woodland near Red Canyon.**

Clockwise from above: **Great blue herons, with a wingspan of almost six feet, are a common sight along Oak Creek. Coyotes are rarely seen but are often heard at night, when packs communicate by yips and howls. Gambel's quail nest in the shade of a prickly-pear cactus, laying up to twenty eggs per clutch.**

Above: Bear grass, or nolina, is not a grass but a member of the lily family.

Left: Mountain lions, though increasingly rare, still roam remote red rock canyons. Mourning doves, named for their melancholy call, are common in neighborhood yards.

Right: Nocturnally active raccoons and javelina often become dependent on the water and food residents leave out for pets and birds.

Common animals, even in town, include ravens, quail, javelina, coyote, and deer. Ravens play "catch-me" and make courtship displays below Sugarloaf, sometimes showing off with a dinner roll swiped from the local KFC. Coyotes serenade the sunset. Plume-topped gambel's quail stop traffic when they parade their walnut-sized chicks across a neighborhood street. Javelina and deer slip into yards at night and

devour everything from tulip bulbs to birdseed. Many homeowners, after finding a rattlesnake dozing in their car-port, or a packrat building a nest in the woodpile, have come to realize that the red rocks are also home to animals—and that the animals were here first.

Not every species has adapted so readily to our presence. The Arizona elk, seen so often in ancient pictographs, were hunted to extinction at the start of the twentieth century. (Today's expanding elk population is descended from Yellowstone imports.) Peregrine falcons and other raptors raise their broods on cliffs that echo with the thunder of helicopters. And consider the unfortunate deer herd that made Airport Mesa their home—after several mishaps, the airstrip was at last fenced off.

Though the desert's prickly plants and feisty critters seem quite able to defend them-selves, Sedona's low-rainfall environment is actually quite fragile. In off-trail areas, a thin cryptobiotic crust holds soil in place, preventing devastating erosion, and many species, such as peregrine falcons, are sensitive to human pres-ence and environmental change. For centuries this land has provided food, shelter, recreation, and inspiration. Treating it with a sense of stewardship and appreciation will help protect it for centuries to come.

Above: **Cottontails eat grasses, mesquite, and cactus. Male tarantulas, docile unless provoked, hide by day but roam at dawn or dusk in search of a mate.** *Pages 16-17:* **A springtime carpet of owl clover stretches below Bear Mountain.**

Sedona's Seasons

Sedona's mild climate makes it a paradise for hikers and others who love to be outdoors. Daytime winter temperatures rarely drop below forty degrees, and even on the hottest July day, mornings and evenings are very comfortable.

Like much of Arizona, Sedona has two rainy seasons. Summer rains begin sometime in mid-July, often as brief afternoon storms followed by brilliant rainbows. Most of the area's annual precipitation of 17 inches falls during this "monsoon" period, which usually ends sometime in September.

October is a glorious month, with warm days and cool nights, perfect for festivals and concerts. From the end of October and well into November, pockets of maple, cottonwood, and sycamore glow with yellow, orange, and red in Oak Creek Canyon.

The winter rainy season, beginning in December, occasionally brings light dustings of snow to the highest peaks. When these winter storms lift, clouds thread in and out of rock spires and buttes, and golden afternoon sunlight highlights cliffs sparkling with fresh-fallen snow.

Though overnight frosts and heavy snows are possible into April, hints of spring will happen as early as February. Manzanita bushes are among the first to bloom, followed by spring wildflowers—purple carpets of owl's clover, delicate white cream cups, bold blue and red spears of larkspur and penstemon.

In May, daytime temperatures begin to climb toward the nineties and the dry summer takes hold. The sky is a deep cloudless blue. Several weeks may pass without a drop of rain. Rock pools dry up, forcing animals closer to town for water. In late June, clouds begin to build every morning on the horizon, fading by afternoon. Some years thunder-and-lightning storms will precede rain, just when the forest is most vulnerable to wildfire.

And then, one day in July, the rains begin again.

Opposite: Bigtooth maples turn brilliant colors each autumn along West Fork, a tributary of Oak Creek. *Above:* A rainbow arches toward Courthouse Butte after a monsoon shower. *Center:* Oak Creek is a summer oasis of vibrant green. *Left:* Winter snows usually melt from all but the highest peaks or deepest canyons by midday. *Pages 20-21:* A fallen, moss-covered ponderosa pine lies along West Fork Trail.

Cultural History

Opposite: **Archaeologist Jesse Walter Fewkes studied the ruins of Palatki (Hopi for Red House) in 1895.** *Above:* **Images on stone mark the passage of earlier cultures.** *Top:* **This pictograph was made by a Sinaguan villager sometime around A.D. 1200.** *Right:* **The Sinagua crafted stone arrow points, cotton cloth, and other items, trading for goods from as far away as the Pacific coast and Mexico.**

PREHISTORY

ABOUT SEVEN YEARS AGO, a graduate student participating in an archaeological study at Honanki ruins west of Sedona slipped away from the rest of the crew to answer nature's call, when he looked down and spotted a piece of worked stone. His serendipitous bathroom break brought to light the first Clovis point found in the red rock area. This point, along with others found since, suggests that early hunter-gatherers roamed the red rock canyons of Sedona as many as ten thousand years ago.

One of the hottest debates in archaeology right now is when and how the first people migrated to the North American continent. Recent finds lead some archaeologists to believe that people have lived in North America for forty thousand years. Still, the most widely accepted theory is that Clovis hunters were the first to migrate from Asia over the Bering Straight some twelve thousand years ago, as ice-age glaciers were receding.

As the climate continued to warm up and dry out, megafauna became extinct. Hunters sought smaller game, such as deer and antelope, and began to make smaller points. Beginning about eight thousand years ago, archaic hunter-gatherers traveled in pursuit of game, moving from one area to the next as the seasons changed and different plants became available as forage for the animals. Like the paleo people before them, archaic hunter-gathers sheltered in caves and rocks and left very little evidence of their passage here in the red rocks—except at Red Cliffs, where they left their marks on the sandstone walls.

The rock markings at Red Cliffs, about fifteen miles northwest of Sedona, provide a fairly complete record of this area's human presence, from pioneer homesteaders all the way back to ancient hunting cultures. One pictograph at Red Cliffs likely depicts an atlatl, a spear thrower used thousands of years ago. Among the oldest rock markings at Red Cliffs are lightly incised geometric petroglyphs, possibly made by paleoindians. Newer, painted-on geometrics are attributed to the archaic period, which lasted until the first millennium.

Because people depended upon the environment for their food, shelter, and clothing needs, technological advances were inextricably linked to the landscape. The most dramatic shift in prehistoric life came when people began to plant crops and tend them. This new lifestyle required year-round dwellings, rather than temporary shelters and camps. Tools for processing food changed as well. Circular grinding stones, used for wild grass seeds, evolved into the rectangular trough metates most efficient for grinding corn.

Images on Stone

About fifteen miles northwest of Sedona, near the long-abandoned Sinaguan village of Palatki, a series of rock alcoves shelters over six thousand images made on stone walls. The site, called Red Cliffs, is an amazing record left by a series of cultures, from ancient hunter-gatherers to Anglo pioneers.

Most of us call prehistoric images on stone "rock art," while some prefer the terms "rock marking" or "rock writing." After all, it is very unlikely that the images were intended as "art" in the decorative sense. They may have recorded events or ceremonies. They may have been used to instruct or enlighten, to identify clans, or to ensure a successful hunt.

In the terminology of rock art, element refers to a specific image or symbol, such as a snake. Anthropomorphs are human-like figures and zoomorphs are animal-like. Geometrics can include weaving patterns, spirals, grids, and so on. Petroglyphs are carved or incised into stone. Pictographs are painted on using a brush, perhaps made from a yucca leaf, and pigments, often ground-up minerals mixed with some kind of binder, such as water or plant sap.

Dating rock art is still an inexact science. To remove organic material from a pictograph for a radiocarbon date, for example, would damage the image. Instead, dates are assigned based on style, relative positioning, and associated artifacts. Archaeological dating methods continue to evolve and improve, which is one reason site conservation is important. Even the oils from someone's fingertips may contaminate the stone and hasten deterioration.

In a sense, places like Red Cliffs are an outdoor museum. The images preserved here give us a precious link to earlier cultures.

This panel of pictographs, probably made with hematite (red) and kaolin (white) pigments, appears to portray game animals and a person with a bow and arrow. Perhaps it was created as a form of "hunting magic." Though we can speculate, we can't be certain what centuries-old images mean. For many people, this mystery is part of rock art's appeal.

These shifts become noticeable in the Sedona area around A.D. 650. People here took to the agricultural way of life relatively slowly compared to other areas in Arizona, probably because of the rich array of resources this area offered. Agave, yucca fruits, walnuts, berries, piñon nuts, amaranth, plantain—these are only a few of the wild-growing foods found here, and people, such as the Sinagua, continued to use them even after they became farmers.

Archaeologists offer different explanations for the development of the agricultural people we refer to as Sinagua. Some theorize that the Sinagua migrated here from other parts of the Southwest. However, Peter Pilles, a Coconino forest archaeologist, believes that their distinct culture arose from surrounding hunter-gatherer peoples. A few Hohokam farmers and traders moved up from the Salt River Valley area

(present-day Phoenix) and influenced the Sinagua, who were also influenced by the Mogollon of the eastern mountains and the Anasazi of northern Arizona.

Harold Colton, who founded the Museum of Northern Arizona in 1928, was the first to identify this culture. He named them Sinagua because they lived around the San Francisco Peaks, which Spanish explorers had dubbed the *Sierra sin Agua* (Mountains without Water).

Early Sinagua homesites were small clusters of pithouses scattered throughout Red Rock Country, most now virtually invisible due to time and erosion. Sinagua farmers raised corn, beans, and squash; made plain pottery of reddish clay; and traded for pots and jewelry with their Hohokam and Anasazi neighbors.

From A.D. 1130 to A.D. 1300, the Sinagua built pueblos of red stone, many of them tucked

"An interpretation presented today may be only one of several possibilities and can be altered dramatically tomorrow by a single piece of new archaeological evidence."

PETER J. PILLES, JR.

"Perhaps a study of their history will help us meet some of our own problems of urbanization and avoid some of the mistakes made by earlier inhabitants."

HAROLD S. COLTON

Opposite: Sinaguan villagers lived in the two-storied cliff dwelling we call Palatki from A.D. 1100-1300. *Top:* Archaeologists have developed a chronology for pottery designs that helps date sites and identify trading partnerships. *Above:* Small masonry dwellings are tucked into alcoves in many red rock canyons. *Below:* Archaeologists study the material remains of earlier cultures in order to better understand how people interacted with their environment and with each other.

into alcoves within hidden red rock canyons. These villages, typified by Honanki and Palatki, were home to groups of related families, or clans. They too left their marks on the sandstone walls of Red Cliffs, painting human and animal figures in white pigment, probably kaolin clay, a local resource and item for trade.

Sometime around A.D. 1300, the Sinagua began to move to hilltop villages near perennial streams, such as Wet Beaver Creek and the Verde River. Prime examples of these villages are Montezuma Castle and Tuzigoot. About five thousand Sinagua lived throughout the area, linked to the north and south by a major trade route, the Palatkwapi trail. They traded expertly woven cottons and other items for goods from as far away as the Pacific coast and Mexico.

Then, little more than a century later, these large hilltop villages were abandoned. Some people might say the Sinagua "mysteriously disappeared." Not so. Today we believe that many Sinagua families left the Verde Valley area and migrated north to Chavez Pass, eventually joining other ancestral puebloan cultures at the Hopi Mesas. Others likely stayed behind and intermarried with the Yavapai people, returning to hunting and gathering as a way of life.

The real mystery is why they left an area so rich in resources. The Sinagua had already weathered the Great Drought that began at the end of the thirteenth century, and the Verde Valley's perennial creeks and rivers continued to flow. Nor was resource depletion a major factor, based on population estimates compared to the availability of potential local farmland. Were the hilltop villages a last line of defense against invaders from elsewhere? Athabaskan peoples, the Navajo and Apache, would not enter the Southwest for another hundred years. It is possible that the large Hohokam population to the south sent raiding parties to the Verde Valley after their canals were destroyed by floods in the late 1300s. However, no signs of all-out warfare have been uncovered by archaeologists.

Many Hopi simply say that it was time for their ancestors, or Hisatsinom, to move on. After all, they had been instructed by the deity Maasaw to leave their footprints all over the Fourth World. Migration was fulfillment of a spiritual duty, their destiny.

Around A.D. 1300, about the same time the Sinagua were moving to their large hilltop villages, the Yavapai people entered the Verde Valley. The Yavapai, Yuman speakers, may be descended from the prehistoric Patayan culture that occupied the Colorado River valley. Remains of Yavapai camps have been found adjacent to Sinagua villages, suggesting that the two lived side-by-side and traded with each other.

The Tonto Apache, Athabaskan speakers, probably did not arrive in the Verde Valley until after 1500. Both the Yavapai and Tonto Apache peoples were nomadic hunter-gathers, and the Sedona area made a rough boundary between their territories.

The branch of Yavapai who roamed throughout this area was the Wipukapaya, "the people of the red rocks." Traveling widely in search of game and wild plants, they relied on lightweight tools such as baskets and small stone arrow points. Both Yavapai and Tonto Apache people built round-topped brush shelters (owas or wickiups) where they would stay for a time to hunt or gather food, such as fresh greens in the spring or prickly-pear fruit ripening in September.

A prized food for the Yavapai (and the Sinagua before them) was the agave, or century plant. Women and children gathered and trimmed the plants while a stone-lined roasting pit was being heated by fire. The plants were loaded into the coals and covered with grasses and earth, and then left to cook for days. The sweet pulp was a delicacy. What couldn't be eaten on the spot was processed by pounding on stones and then dried, becoming a valuable trade item. The reddish-brown juices could be used as face paint. Strong fibers from agave leaves were twisted together for cordage, which was then used to make baskets, mats, and rope.

The large roasting pit at Red Cliffs is sheltered in a theater-like alcove, its walls covered by pictographs, many of them Yavapai. Picture these walls at night, flickering with firelight, as people gathered to tell stories, exchange news, and perhaps meet a potential spouse. High above the entrance to the alcove, images of akaka—little beings associated with rocky places and imbued with special powers—stand guard, perhaps to help with ceremonies. . .or to warn participants to be on their best behavior.

Other Yavapai pictographs at Red Cliffs include quartered circles, a symbol they also incorporated in jewelry and tattoos. To the Spanish explorers who journeyed through the Verde Valley in the late 1500s, the symbol looked like an encircled cross, and they referred to the Yavapai as the *pueblo del cruzado* (people of the cross). The Spanish soldiers and priests rode on, perhaps believing the Yavapai were already Christianized or, more likely, because they didn't find the silver and gold they were seeking.

Trappers and scouts traveled through the area in the early 1800s, but they also did not stay. Then, in 1863, gold was discovered near Prescott. Farmers, ranchers, and merchants quickly followed the miners, and lands the Yavapai had used seasonally and communally

were fenced and plowed. Conflict was inevitable, and settlers petitioned the government for military aid. Fort Verde's precursor, Camp Lincoln, was established in 1865.

Between the years of 1871-1873, while General George Crook was in command at Fort Verde, over a thousand Yavapai and Apache were relocated to the Rio Verde Reservation. Years of struggle and hardship ensued. Finally, around the turn of the century when most of the animosity subsided, many Yavapai families returned to the Verde Valley. By this time, Jerome was a mining boomtown and Sedona a growing farming community. Fort Verde, once a linchpin in Arizona's Indian campaigns, had stood abandoned for more than a decade. Even though the Yavapai were once again in their homeland, their traditional lifestyle had vanished forever.

Left: Prehistoric people shaped pottery according to function, using pots for cooking, serving, storing food, and carrying water.

Above: After twenty-five years or more, the agave plant sends up a tall stalk that can grow inches in a single day. It flowers in late spring, attracting insects and hummingbirds to its blooms, and then dies. Native peoples had over a hundred uses for the agave, from food to fiber to medicine. *Right:* The alcoves and overhangs at Red Cliffs have sheltered people for thousands of years.

Pages 30-31: Oak Creek provided a seasonal bounty of acorns, walnuts, berries, watercress, and other wild foods for prehistoric people and the Anglo settlers who followed.

PIONEERS

Opposite: **The waters of Oak Creek attracted Anglo settlers in the late 1800s.** *Above:* **J. J. Thompson was the first to claim land in Oak Creek Canyon, building a pair of log cabins on a ranch he called Indian Gardens and raising nine children.** *Below:* **For many years, cattle were more common than cars on the road between Sedona and Bell Rock, now Hwy. 179.**

Oak Creek Canyon today is a popular recreation area drawing hikers, swimmers, and fisherfolk to its clear waters and hiking trails. During the height of autumn's leaf-peeping season or in the midst of spring break, looking for a place to pull over on the winding two-lane road can be difficult at best.

But wander down a curve in the creek, where rushing water is the only sound and the canopy of sycamores and cottonwoods screens out signs of modern life, and it's possible to imagine the lonely paradise that Jim Thompson encountered a century and a quarter ago. Native trout leapt and splashed in the creek's crystal waters. Narrow game trails marked the passage of deer and bear. Plants, from blackberries to watercress, grew in abundance.

It was 1876, and only months earlier, soldiers from Fort Verde thirty miles to the south, had forcefully rounded up bands of Tonto Apache and Yavapai, marching them to the San Carlos Reservation in eastern Arizona, opening the area for the Anglo settlement. A few yards from the creek, an Indian family's garden stood untended, with corn, beans, and squash still growing. Thompson claimed squatter's rights and named his new paradise Indian Gardens Ranch. It provided everything an able young man needed…except companionship.

Hoping for congenial neighbors, Thompson wrote to a family he'd met while he was a ferryman on the Colorado River. In 1879, the Abraham James family settled further down the creek at what is today Crimson Cliffs. Their daughter Margaret married Thompson in 1880 when she was sixteen and he was in his late thirties. Because his cabin at Indian Gardens was remote and difficult to get to, he built another cabin further south, near present-day Uptown, where Maggie and the children stayed when he was gone selling farm goods or game.

The same year Thompson claimed Indian Gardens Ranch, a man named John Lee settled farther down Oak Creek near Cathedral Rock. With the eventual arrival of the Schuerman, Dumas, Huckaby, Armijo, and other farming and ranching families, the area became known as Red Rock.

Henry Schuerman was a German baker who immigrated to Quebec, then journeyed West. He established himself in Prescott as a hotelier, where he wrote to Dorette, his childhood sweetheart in Germany, asking her to join him. In 1884, the newlyweds bought a wagon and team and traveled five days to a 160-acre farm Schuerman had acquired as settlement for a $500 debt. The "farm" had a cabin and a rough irrigation ditch but little else to recommend it other than the views.

And so Dorette Schuerman, who did not yet speak English, found herself not the wife of a prestigious hotelier in Arizona's capitol but the partner of a would-be farmer on an isolated plot of land. With hard work and the help of their neighbors, the Schuermans planted orchards and a vineyard and built a road. By 1891, there were enough children in the Red Rock neighborhood to establish the first local school.

When this part of territorial Arizona was finally surveyed and they could at last apply for homestead rights, the Schuermans discovered their land was actually owned by the railroad. They had to buy it again in 1893, paying the Atlantic & Pacific $400. By this time, they had literally sunk roots into the red soil. And with the rapid growth of Jerome, destined shortly to become one of Arizona's largest cities, the Schuermans and other local homesteaders had a growing market for their produce and livestock.

In 1901, another couple settled between Oak Creek Canyon and Red Rock. Their name was Schnebly, and they soon built a two-story frame house along the creek at the site of the present-day Los Abrigados resort. They had purchased their land from the Owenbys, who were the first to patent land in the area.

The Schnebly house stood at the end of the Munds Trail, the route farmers and ranchers used to transport cattle and goods up to Flagstaff.

The trip took several days, and many stayed at the Schnebly home to break the journey. T. C. "Carl" Schnebly saw a need for a store and mail service, so in 1902 he applied to the government for a post office at "Schnebly Station," only to be told the name was too long for a cancellation stamp. His brother Ellsworth suggested he use his wife's name, and so the little town became Sedona.

Sadly, Carl and Sedona Schnebly left the community in 1905 after their eight-year-old daughter Pearl was killed horseback riding. The girl was buried next to the Schnebly home, and Sedona grew so despondent that the family doctor recommended a move. They left their home and orchards and didn't return until 1929. By this time, travelers had begun to refer to the Munds Trail as the Schnebly Hill Road, and the name stayed even after the Schneblys left their land by the creek.

Clockwise, from top left: A school built in Oak Creek Canyon in 1897 stood halfway between the Thompson and Purtyman claims—all students but one were Thompsons or Purtymans. Carl and Sedona Schneblys' two-story frame house was a place to pick up mail, buy supplies, share a meal, or spend the night. A later Sedona post office still stands today in Uptown. Orchards once stretched from present-day Jordan Road to the creek. Sedona Arabella Miller Schnebly was known to friends and family as "Dona."

Top: **Frank Pendley's orchard still produces apples at Slide Rock State Park.** *Above:* **Helen Jordan and her husband George sold produce from a small store at the north end of Uptown.** *Right:* **Fruit raised in Sedona won prizes at the state fair and fed troops during WWII.**

Later owners, the Blacks, sold the property to W. A. Jordan, whose Bridgeport farm had failed when toxic fumes from the Clarkdale smelter destroyed his crops. His sons George and Walter joined him, Walter taking over the Thompson place along present-day Jordan Road. The Jordans started with strawberries and vegetables, and then built an irrigation ditch so they could add apples and peaches. It took them two years to blast the ditch from the mouth of Wilson Canyon (where Midgely Bridge is today) to their packing barn. George later dug a well that became the town's first water system.

When the Great Depression arrived in the 1930s, Sedona's small farms and orchards were hard hit. Local farmers formed a cooperative, delivering their produce to the Jordan packing barn. From there, George Jordan delivered Sedona-grown produce to Cottonwood, Clarkdale, Jerome, Flagstaff, Williams, and as far away as Holbrook and Phoenix. Though

homesteaders in Oak Creek Canyon had worked together to complete the route to Flagstaff in 1914, it was more trail than road, crossing the creek a dozen times as it wound its way up two thousand feet to the Mogollon Rim. Jordan would leave Sedona long before dawn, prepared for breakdowns with spare parts packed among the produce.

The Purtymans and other canyon families knew how to celebrate the Fourth of July. Afternoon picnics led to all-night dances on a platform made from pine logs, with music, fireworks, and sometimes even a little dynamite. Partygoers didn't head home until daylight.

In later years, Jordan said, "You know, when I think back on all the hard work I did, and remember all the hardships we had, I shudder, and wonder how I managed, but at the time I didn't mind at all."

Despite the hard times, or perhaps because of them, the small community grew even closer. On Saturday nights, people from all over the area gathered for dances at the Brewer Road School. Frank Derrick and Walter Van Deren played fiddle, and Jess Purtyman and Albert Thompson added accordions. Women brought potluck dishes for a midnight supper, and outside, coffee brewed over the fire in a fifty-pound lard can. After the break, dancing would resume, sometimes lasting until dawn, while children slept on benches pushed up against the wall.

Imagine the delight of the local farmers' daughters when the dancers included members of the Civilian Conservation Corps (CCC). In the late thirties, the CCC housed two to three hundred young men in barracks on the site of the present-day King's Ransom Inn. CCC crew member Andy Owens recalled some of their tasks, including fighting forest fires, planting trees, working on Schnebly Hill Road, building cattle fences, and making signs for campgrounds.

J. J. Thompson: First White Settler

Oak Creek Canyon's first white settler was a self-sufficient young man who'd tried cowboying, soldiering, farming, freighting, and ferrying. Jim Thompson's story is a good example of the mettle and hard work it took to settle the West.

He fled Ireland's potato famine when he was only twelve years old. Penniless, he befriended a man who paid his passage to the States. In New York, he met a boy his age whose father was a ship's captain. No doubt dreaming of cowboys and adventure, they stowed away on a ship headed for Texas, where Thompson was adopted by a family in Refugio. He left at sixteen for Mexico, where he learned the cowboying trade. He returned to the States, joined the Rebel army, was wounded and captured, and spent time in a Union prison.

After the Civil War, like so many young men, he headed for California's gold fields. And like many would-be prospectors who arrived too late for the big strike, he ended up traveling on to Arizona looking for the next one. He met the Alexander James family while he was ferrying miners, settlers, and goods across the Colorado River at the Virgin River confluence.

From there, he freighted a load of salt to Prescott, the territorial capitol, and traded for shingles, which he took to the little farm town of Phoenix, finally winding up in Page Springs. One day, he and a friend went upstream to Oak Creek Canyon on a fishing trip. By this time, Thompson was thirty years old and had spent over half a lifetime wandering. But the canyon worked its magic, and he settled down at last.

Hollywood in Arizona?

Why did the fledgling movie industry end up in southern California instead of northern Arizona? Blame Mother Nature.

In 1913, pioneer movie boss Jesse Laske sent young Cecil B. DeMille by train to scout a location for an upcoming Western. Flagstaff seemed perfect…until the worst snowstorm in fifty years shocked the crew and sent them scurrying west to Los Angeles.

Thanks to writer Zane Grey, Laske's company returned to the area in 1923 to film *Call of the Canyon* at West Fork. Five army trucks loaded with equipment slowly made their way down the switchbacks to The Tioga Lodge, built on the site of Bear Howard's homestead. It was the first movie filmed in the Sedona area, and it might have been the last. Once again, Mother Nature didn't cooperate, sending a flash flood that washed out roads and stranded the crew. Laske made the best of the situation, adding a flood scene to the movie. Nevertheless, many years would pass before Hollywood returned to the Sedona area.

MOVIES

I N SEDONA, AS ELSEWHERE, entertainment helped lighten hearts during hard times. But when the movies came to Sedona, they also brought needed employment. Locals found jobs as cooks, wranglers, and extras in such films as *Riders of the Purple Sage* (1931), *Robber's Roost* (1933), and *Dodge City* (1939).

By the mid-forties, several Westerns were being filmed here each year, giving the rest of the world a look at Sedona's red rocks, though the setting was inevitably identified as Wyoming, Montana, New Mexico, or California—and even the home of the Canadian Mounted Police. For that movie, *Pony Soldier* (1952), cactus and yucca were stripped from scenes and replaced by a small forest of ponderosa pines hauled down from Flagstaff.

When John Wayne decided to film *Angel and the Badman* (1946) in Sedona, a flurry of building ensued, including the construction of a soundstage for interior scenes. The old CCC barracks were converted into a lodge and mess hall for cast and crew, and a Western town set was built near Coffee Pot Rock at Grasshopper Flats, an empty expanse of land stretching below Capitol Butte.

When, in 1948, the first well was dug in the Flats by a man named Williams, a real estate boom followed, and West Sedona was the result. "The face and form of Carl E. Williams

should be carved into the towering red walls above what once was the…one-pump village of Sedona," wrote Prescott historian Budge Ruffner.

The outside world intruded more and more on this small community once isolated by rough roads and lack of water. Nevertheless, life in Sedona was so quiet that one old-timer quipped, "You could always start a rumor and chase it up the canyon."

One place where locals could chase rumors and rub elbows with stars was the "Bird Bar." Oma and Lee Bird's Oak Creek Market and Tavern opened in 1945 and became a community center. A couple decades later, the Bird's tavern was used for a scene in *The Rounders* (1964), starring Glenn Ford and Henry Fonda.

Some 250 locals worked as extras in the movie, which featured a parade through Uptown and a rodeo at Posse Grounds. Many scenes were filmed in the Big Park area (later the Village of Oak Creek), where wide open spaces made an ideal backdrop for a movie about cowboy life. The film is notable for being the very first to refer to the town of Sedona by name. The Verde Valley Independent marked the occasion with the headline: "Sedona Finally Called Sedona."

Top Left and Above: **Over eighty movies have been made in the Sedona area, many of them during the golden age of Westerns. Among the finest are John Wayne's** *Angel and the Badman* **(Top left) and** *The Rounders* **(Above), with Henry Fonda and Glenn Ford. Even today, traffic occasionally comes to a standstill while cameras roll for a commercial, television episode, or feature film.** *Top Right:* **Call of the Canyon Resort, once a popular retreat, was named after the first movie filmed in Sedona.**

Contemporary Sedona

RED ROCK LIFESTYLE

SEDONA'S RED ROCKS HAVE LONG inspired dreamers—pioneers who came West and tamed a wild country to raise fruit, cattle, and families; actors and directors who brought Western myths to the big screen; and artists who paid homage to those myths and created new ones. From Sunday painters and struggling sculptors to celebrated artists, many found their muse in the red rocks.

In 1946, influential artist Max Ernst and his wife settled along Brewer Road. The prolific Ernst had experimented with collage, painting, and sculpture, inspiring Europe's Dada and Surrealist movements. He created the sculpture Capricorn at his Sedona home before returning to Paris in 1953, renting his house to Nassan Gobran, an Egyptian sculptor. Gobran came to Sedona to teach and wound up energizing the local art scene.

By this time, the small community of farmers and ranchers had caught the attention of movers and shakers, people of wealth and influence who vacationed or lived here. In the late 1940s, Hamilton Warren founded the Verde Valley School, a private boarding school in the Big Park area, and contacted Gobran to launch the school's art department. After moving to the Ernst home a few years later, Gobran quit working at the school, intending instead to pursue his own art. But he ended up pursuing another vision altogether, that of establishing an art colony in Sedona.

With the help of an art supply store owner, Gobran launched summer art classes that attracted students and professionals from all over the United States. The summer art colony was the seed of the Sedona Arts Center, whose founding members included the Warrens, George Babbitt of the prominent Flagstaff family, Marguerite Staude (heiress and builder of the Chapel of the Holy Cross), and artist Helen Varner Frye (designer of the fabulous House of Apache Fire). But the young organization needed a permanent home.

Though Walter Jordan, Frank Pendley, and other local farmers continued to raise apples, George Jordan's old apple-packing barn had stood empty for years. The owner offered to rent it to Gobran for $25 a month, and after months of renovation and preparations, the Sedona Arts Center (SAC) held its first show on April 28, 1961. SAC became the center of Sedona's cultural life with classes, concerts, plays, dinners, costume parties, and of course, art shows.

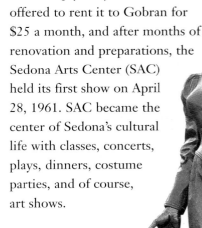

Opposite: **West Sedona is primarily a residential area, with schools, grocery stores, and offices, as well as restaurants, shops, and motels.**
Above: **A hiker enjoys a moment of solitude in Boynton Canyon.**
Right: **Local artist Susan Kliewer's graceful bronze sculpure of Sedona Schnebly stands at the door of the community library.**

Over forty years have passed since Gobran's summer art colony began in 1958, with SAC's membership growing to fifteen hundred artists and patrons. Local and visiting artists teach nearly two hundred classes a year—painting, pottery, weaving, and more—in the old apple barn, SAC's new building, or in area schools.

One of SAC's founders had an artistic vision of another sort. Marguerite Staude, a sculptor, had long dreamed of building a church dedicated to art. In 1955, she braved a plane for the first time in order to survey potential building sites from the air. She settled on a spur of rock in what was then known as Little Horse Park. Thanks to her friend Senator Barry Goldwater, the permit process for building on forest service land was expedited. But when construction supervisor Fred Coukos saw the site, he said, "I almost turned around and went home."

Instead, Coukos moved his family to Sedona and went to work, building retaining walls and moving at least twenty-five tons of rock without dynamite. The Chapel of the Holy Cross was completed eighteen months later at a cost of only $300,000. The chapel gained the attention of the national press, including Life magazine and the New York Times, and won awards for its austere yet serene beauty. It was one of

Sedona's few attractions in the early 1960s when residents numbered a couple thousand.

"I couldn't understand why more people hadn't heard about Sedona," said real estate agent Edith Geary, who moved here in 1961, "but it was because the people in Flagstaff considered Sedona their special place, and they did not tell anyone about it." Geary helped begin the Sedona West subdivision, where the Coffee Pot movie set once stood. "You could also go outside and stand on the hill and only count six lights at night, because that's all there were in West Sedona."

Sedona's reputation as art community and vacation retreat continued to grow, and in 1966 the area's first luxury resort, Poco Diablo, was built. It was a new page in the town's long history of hospitality that began with the Schneblys, who sheltered travelers in their home not long after the turn of the century. But the small-town atmosphere lingered on.

In the meantime, a couple miles north of the resort, something truly wonderful and mysterious was happening behind an adobe wall along Hwy. 179. Abe Miller began constructing a Spanish colonial-style arts-and-crafts village in 1971, a place where artists could live and work under towering sycamore trees.

Top: The Chapel of the Holy Cross, completed in 1956, is made of reinforced concrete aggregate and built directly into the sandstone cliffs. *Above and opposite:* Tlaquepaque's traditional architecture includes balconies, iron grillwork, hidden niches, ceramic tile, archways, and courtyards such as this one, where candlelit luminarias enchant holiday visitors.

Left: The fountains and floral displays at Tlaquepaque are a backdrop to numerous festivals. *Bottom:* Weavers from throughout the Navajo Nation sell their work at Garland's Navajo Rugs. *Opposite:* Though Sedona's nightlife includes theatre, concerts, and dance clubs, many visitors prefer the small-town quiet and dark, star-studded skies.

Tlaquepaque was completed in 1978, after years of painstaking work that honored traditional techniques, building around trees in order to create a centuries-old ambiance.

Today, Tlaquepaque is home to over forty shops, restaurants, and galleries, but it remains much more than a shopping center. It is an architectural wonder of exquisite detail, a summer oasis of beautiful gardens and fountains, and a year-round gathering place with lively festivals and enticing farmers' markets. On one very special evening every December, visitors and residents participate in lighting over a thousand luminaries that make courtyards and staircases glow.

No wonder so many of Sedona's visitors decided to stay. To meet the needs of a growing population, the area's first large grocery store opened in West Sedona in 1971. Four years later, the first movie theater opened—ironic considering that Sedonans had long been in the movies as doubles and extras, but had to go to the schoolhouse or a motel parking lot to see the movies.

Sometime after tourism replaced apples as the town's leading industry, a very enterprising person erected a "hippie teepee" on a vacant lot and began selling beads and trinkets. That empty spot is long gone, and Uptown Sedona is now home to dozens of shops and galleries, with dozens more on Hwy. 179's Gallery Row. Paintings and sculpture; locally designed clothing; Native American jewelry, pottery,

rugs, and kachinas; crafts with Sedona themes made by local artisans—all can be found in Sedona's eighty-plus galleries and countless shops.

About the same time business was picking up in the 1960s and 1970s, there were stirrings of another sort. Sedona's starry skies garnered lots of attention in May 1975, when the local paper reported two incidents of odd celestial sightings. One local resident likened it to "a Michelob beer bottle turned upside down." Thanks to a recent dark sky ordinance, Sedona's skies continue to be a great place to watch for stars…and whatever else might be out there.

Earth Energy

Around 1980, a local psychic channeled information from an entity named Albion regarding areas of powerful energy in the Sedona area. Today, the curious can find varying answers to their questions about Sedona's vortex phenomenon in books, from lectures, or on guided tours. Perhaps the simplest explanation comes from author Dennis Andres, who says, "A vortex is a place in nature where the Earth is exceptionally alive and healthy."

Most everyone agrees that four major vortices exist in the Sedona area, at Bell Rock, Cathedral Rock, Boynton Canyon, and the Airport Mesa saddle. They have been variously described as electric, magnetic, masculine, feminine, amplifiers of thought or emotion, and beacons of communication to other parts of the universe.

But no matter how you describe them, even the most skeptical person would have to agree that these are places of exquisite beauty, where taking a few moments to sit quietly is its own reward.

Some date the beginning of Sedona's New Age phenomenon to the 1980s, when vortex sites were "discovered" and the Harmonic Convergence attracted thousands of seekers. Yet here, as elsewhere, the New Age is anything but new. Vortex theories are based on old traditions of geomancy, or earth energies. Throw in respect for such venerable world traditions as Native American spirituality, shamanism, Christianity, Buddhism, and Sufism, as well as ages-old healing practices like acupuncture and Ayurveda, and you have a mixture that is right at home in the red rocks. Free thinkers and religious communities have found spiritual solace here for decades.

Many bookstores, tour companies, workshops, classes, and retreats cater to spiritual seekers. It's possible to begin the day with a vortex hike or yoga class in the red rocks, enjoy an energizing massage or attunement in the afternoon, and then spend a relaxing evening participating in a group meditation or drumming circle under the stars. Events and offerings are advertised in local papers and posted on bookstore bulletin boards.

Though skeptics—and adherents—poke fun at some aspects of the New Age, the movement's bottom line is about self-discovery and expanding one's awareness. And what better place to do so than among Sedona's red rocks and green woodlands? As John Muir once said, "The clearest way into the Universe is through a forest wilderness."

Top: The spires of Cathedral Rock are considered a vortex.

Above: A recent survey found that over sixty percent of visitors come to Red Rock Country seeking some sort of spiritual experience.

Festivals and Fun

Right: The Georgia Frontiere Performing Arts Pavilion at the Sedona Cultural Park hosts numerous concerts and festivals from spring through fall. *Below:* Festivals at Tlaquepaque highlight the traditional music, dance, and artistry of Southwestern cultures.

Spring kicks off in March with the annual Sedona International Film Festival, screening more than fifty independent films. For history buffs, March is also Archaeology Awareness Month, with programs offered throughout the state, including Red Rock State Park and Palatki/Red Cliffs. May brings the Sedona Fine Arts Festival, the Northern Arizona Watercolor Society's annual exhibit, and a busy concert season, beginning with the Latin Jazz Festival and concerts hosted by Chamber Music Sedona and the Phoenix Symphony.

June's architecture and art tour offers an inside look at local residences. The Sedona Arts Center (SAC) holds its annual member show, and local restaurants dish up culinary delights at the Sedona Taste. The Fourth of July gala is an all-American, small-town celebration with fireworks and local bands. The Shakespeare Sedona theatre group performs in July and August. During Moonlight Madness, Uptown shops stay open late and sidewalk booths offer food and entertainment.

Fall events include the venerable Jazz on the Rocks festival, Jackson Browne's concert to benefit Native American scholarships, and the colorful Fiesta del Tlaquepaque—all in September. Early October brings SAC's prestigious Sculpture Walk, followed by the Sedona Arts Festival and the EcoFest, a full day of music and art in celebration of the environment.

SAC's annual miniature show is held early in November. Later in the month, Red Rock Fantasy opens with a holiday spectacular of over a million twinkling lights and fifty displays that continue into January. Other holiday events include Santa's arrival, capped by a tree lighting in Uptown, and

Tlaquepaque's stirring Festival of Lights. Chamber Music Sedona brightens the winter months with several concerts in January and February.

For information about these and other events, contact the Sedona–Oak Creek Chamber of Commerce at 800-288-7336 or 928-282-7722, or visit the following websites:

www.sedonaculturalpark.org
www.sedona.jazz.com
www.chambermusicsedona.org
www.tlaq.com
www.sedona.net

For nature lovers, there's a lot to love—160,000 acres of public land, from canyon to creek to mountaintop, with a half-dozen public campgrounds, numerous picnic areas, challenging slickrock slopes for mountain bikers, and more than sixty hiking trails, all inviting a deeper experience with this magical landscape. Scenic drives lead to inspiring views and special places, and state parks offer programs and ranger-led hikes that teach about wildlife and history.

A good way for first-time visitors to get their bearings is to take a trolley tour of the city and its environs. Or, start with the short but scenic drive up Airport Mesa, where you'll find two overlooks, a challenging hiking trail, a vortex, and access to commercial air tour companies.

RECREATION

WHETHER YOU SEEK SPIRITUAL renewal or just plain fun, there are plenty of opportunities for both in Sedona. But where to start? With so many ways to see the red rocks, trying to choose can be the hardest part.

It's possible to get a hawk's eye view from a hot air balloon, helicopter, or airplane, or explore by horseback, stagecoach, trolley, Hummer, or Hawg. If renting a Harley-Davidson motorcycle isn't your thing, you can zip around town on a Vespa scooter à la Audrey Hepburn in *Roman Holiday*. And perhaps the most popular way to explore Red Rock Country is with a commercial jeep tour. Routes include thrilling rides up and down sandstone ledges, privately guided vortex experiences, and trips to Sinaguan ruins or a pioneer homestead.

Sedona's many resorts, from luxurious to rustic, offer health spas, creekside retreats, tennis courts, and golf courses. If you choose golf, be ready for a new kind of hazard—the views can be distracting. Sedona Golf Resort's No. 10 hole is considered to be the most photographed in Arizona. Gary Panks designed the course to take advantage of the natural topography, as well as the views.

For another easy drive, take Hwy. 179 south to the Village of Oak Creek. The road passes the Chapel of the Holy Cross and winds between beautiful red and buff cliffs before reaching the Village, where Bell Rock and Courthouse Butte tower over desert grasslands. The highway continues underneath the I-17 interchange to the Wet Beaver Creek campground and picnic area and the fascinating V-V Ranch petroglyph site.

Opposite: **Oak Creek attracts swimmers, anglers, hikers, and birdwatchers.**

Clockwise from top: **A hot air balloon floats toward Cockscomb. Sedona's golf courses feature views with the fairways. Mountain bike routes include rugged forest roads and slickrock expanses. Jeep tours head into Sedona's backcountry for fabulous vistas.**

Opposite: Slide Rock State Park is a favorite for families, offering swimming, picnicking, and hiking. *Above:* Trails on Munds Mountain give hikers an up-close look at the geology of Red Rock Country. *Below:* Broken Arrow can be explored by foot, mountain bike, or jeep.

Hwy. 89A through Oak Creek Canyon was America's first officially designated scenic byway. Swimming holes, picnic areas, campgrounds, motels, B&Bs, and resorts line the creek on its fourteen-mile path up the canyon. Grasshopper Point and Call of the Canyon day-use areas offer creekside picnicking and hiking. To the delight of fisherfolk, the creek is regularly stocked with trout. Slide Rock State Park, six miles north of Sedona, is famous for its natural water slide through a sandstone chute. It's on the site of the historic Pendley Ranch, where Frank Pendley and his nine children tended one of the area's most successful apple orchards.

Sunbathers and swimmers congregate along the creek from spring break through September. In October and November, leaf-peeping is a favorite activity. And after a winter snowfall, the canyon is a wonderland of white—but also a treacherous drive.

Schnebly Hill Road winds up to the Mogollon Rim past gorgeous Mitten Ridge and Merry-Go-Round Rock. The views are unparalleled, though the road is primitive. Unless you have a high-clearance vehicle, it's best to experience this area with a jeep tour, mountain bike, or on foot via the Munds Wagon Trail. For a look at Sedona's backcountry, take paved Dry Creek Road to Boynton Canyon (about three miles) or to Boynton Pass via FR 152C, a bumpy dirt road.

Sedona's sensuous beauty can't be fully appreciated through a windshield, however. Forest roads and many hiking trails can also be traveled by mountain bike (note that bikes are not allowed in wilderness areas). Local bike shops offer rentals, as well as the latest information on trails. It's a good idea to start by getting acclimated to the heat, elevation, and dry climate with an easy route, such the Bell Rock Pathway, before graduating to a bigger challenge, like the Jim Thompson or Broken Arrow Trails. Save longer rides, like the route to the top of House Mountain, an extinct volcano, until you're certain of your stamina and skill level.

Red Rock Loop Road, west of Sedona, begins and ends on Hwy. 89A. Drive down the upper loop for gorgeous views of Cathedral Rock. A left turn on Chavez Ranch Road leads to the Crescent Moon day-use area, a great place to picnic, soak in the creek, or photograph Cathedral Rock's graceful spires. On the lower loop, Red Rock State Park has hiking trails and an education center with programs and displays on the riparian ecosytem. Ranger-guided hikes lead to the historic House of Apache Fire and focus on birdwatching, wildflowers, geology, and astronomy.

The same goes for hiking—start with an easy trail and stop often. There's a lot to take in besides the views: the heady scent of cliffrose, the descending notes of a canyon wren's call, the delicate lacework of lizard tracks in pink sand. Trails curve through shady cypress forests and along sheer sandstone cliffs, passing below ancient ruins tucked into alcoves or leading up to ledges with astonishing vistas.

In upper Oak Creek Canyon, the popular West Fork Trail—some call it Sedona's premier hike—winds underneath a canopy of bigtooth maples, boxelder, and conifers as it follows a tributary of Oak Creek. The trail starts at Call of the Canyon day-use area, once the site of the Mayhew's Lodge and the first movie filmed in the Sedona area.

Most day hikers turn around before the 3-mile point, though the canyon continues north, 12 miles in all. Deep blue-green pools, which are set like chilly jewels between sheer stone cliffs, challenge backpackers seeking to explore the canyon's full length. (To protect the canyon's riparian ecosystem, no camping is allowed within the first six miles.)

West Fork Trail is delightful spring through fall, with wildflowers and hanging gardens, a crystal-clear stream, pools and passages sculpted from sandstone, and splashes of autumn color.

Several Oak Creek trails were built by pioneers to transport goods from the canyon's east rim down to their creekside cabins. One pioneer route, the Jim Thompson Trail, begins at the end of Jordan Road north of Uptown. Thompson built this trail to his cabin at Indian Gardens with a pickaxe and a shovel. The moderately easy 2.4-mile trail cuts through a cypress forest and skirts the cliffs of Steamboat Rock, where ravens play tag with their shadows. High above, the "sail" of Ship Rock angles down to the red spires known as Solomon and his Three Sisters, with Uptown's shops and homes gently nestled below.

The trail offers a raven's eye look at Midgely Bridge before connecting with the Wilson Mountain Trail, a challenging 5.6-mile climb to Sedona's highest peak (over seven thousand feet).

The Brin's Mesa and Jordan Trails also begin at the end of Jordan Road. Brin's Mesa, named after a wily brindle-colored bull, is a high tableland that overlooks red rock canyons, buttes, and spires. The trail begins in a forest of manzanita bushes, and as the 3.2-mile trail climbs toward the mesa, sharp-eyed hikers will spot the Teapot, Earth Angel Spire, Snoopy, and other well-known formations. The last mile is a steep, rocky climb to the top, where panoramic views and seasonal surprises—perhaps an ephemeral waterfall plunging down the cliffs—await.

Just a short mile up Schnebly Hill Road, a picnic area offers access to the Huckaby and the Munds Wagon Trails. The Munds Wagon Trail retraces a route used by the pioneer Munds family to travel between their Verde Valley ranch and the cooler summer pastures of the Mogollon Rim. Now recently restored, the 4-mile Munds Wagon Trail climbs from the base of Bear Wallow Canyon, circles Merry-Go-Round Rock, and ends at a rim vista. It's a stress-free foot-powered alternative to the notorious, oil pan–busting drive up Schnebly Hill Road.

The Huckaby Trail heads north to Midgely Bridge or south to the Marg's Draw Trail. This trail, in turn, connects with the Broken Arrow Trail. With the help of local and national volunteer crews, the forest service plans to connect several trails, over twenty miles in all, that will encircle the city through its "neighborwoods."

Right: Maroon Mountain's twin peaks rise above Sedona's backcountry, where hikers might see bear scat or mountain lion tracks along trails such as the Vultee Arch Trail.

Opposite: Drive, bike, or hike up Schnebly Hill for views from Bear Wallow Canyon all the way to the Black Hills. *Right:* The 43,950-acre Red Rock–Secret Mountain Wilderness Area includes high cliffs, deep canyons, and erosion-carved arches and spires.

If Marg's Draw and Broken Arrow inspire a sense of déja vu, you might be having a Sedona experience. Or, you may have been here before, thanks to Hollywood. The Crimson Cliffs near Snoopy Rock and the cypress-filled valley below Munds Mountain were the backdrop for several scenes in the 1950 Jimmy Stewart film *Broken Arrow.* Today, the 2-mile Broken Arrow Trail is a favorite of mountain bikers and parallels a popular jeep route to Chicken Point. Along the trail is Devil's Dining Room, a seventy-five foot deep sinkhole cavern created when underlying Redwall limestone dissolved away.

Further south, the Village of Oak Creek also has several trailheads, including the easy 3-mile Bell Rock Pathway, which connects to the Courthouse Butte Loop. Both trails give hikers up-close views of Bell Rock, said to be a "masculine" vortex.

West of Sedona, a dozen trails lead into the Red Rock–Secret Mountain Wilderness Area. FR 152 (off Dry Creek Road) is locally known as the Vultee Arch Road. This primitive dirt road leads to four trailheads, with access to twice that many trails. The Devil's Bridge Trail is under a mile, with a moderately challenging climb to a sandstone arch.

The view from the arch takes in the Dry Creek basin, Sedona's backcountry. During most of the year the basin's washes are as dry as the creek, but centuries of springtime floods have sculpted chutes and tubs into Dry Creek's bedrock base, creating pools of water that attract coyote, deer, and other animals between rains.

At the end of Dry Creek Road, the dirt-surfaced Boynton Pass Road heads west (left) to Fay Canyon, Bear Mountain, and lovely Doe Mesa. A right turn leads to Enchantment Resort. The site of this elegant resort was once the home of a stockman named Boeington, who eked out a living capturing and selling wild horses. He wintered his herd in this box canyon now known as Boynton Canyon.

The popular Boynton Canyon Trail is a walk into another world. This is the Yavapai tribe's place of emergence, where Skatakaampcha lived with his grandmother, Old Woman Rock. Centuries later, new age visionaries identified it as a vortex. Not far from the canyon's entrance a short side trail leads up to Kachina Woman, the spire many claim to be the source of Boynton Canyon's calming energy.

The natural landscape of Sedona is waiting for those who are prepared to explore with an open mind and heart. It's possible to fill each day with a multitude of activities, or to spend a whole day just sitting on a rock, watching the colors shift as the sun moves through the sky. In either case, your adventure will take you deeper into the mystery of this incredible landscape.

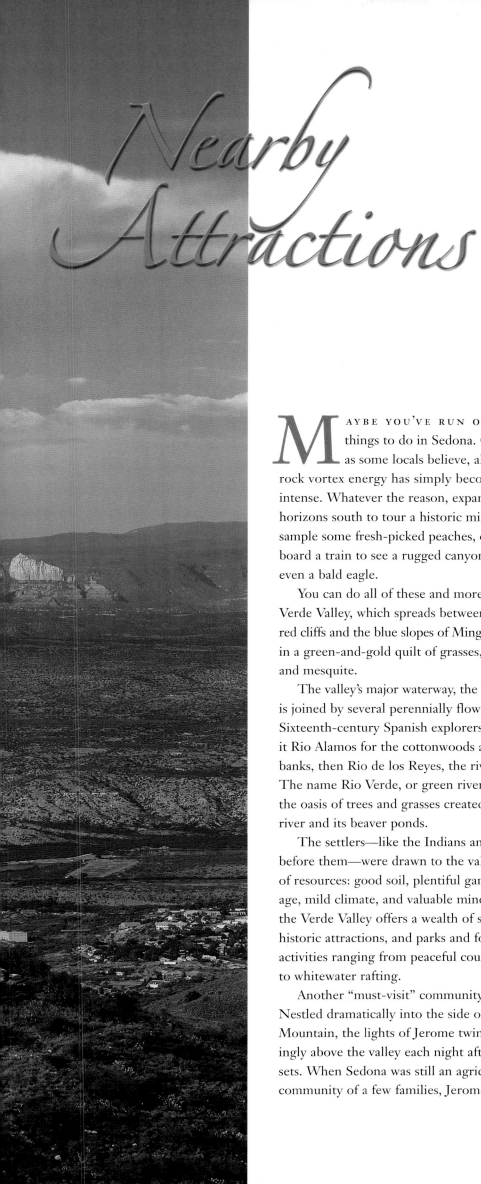

Nearby Attractions

wicked mining boomtown, with a population that peaked at fifteen thousand in the 1920s.

Boardinghouse rooms were occupied in shifts corresponding to miners' hours. Brush wickiups dotted the Hogback near engineers' houses, where Yavapai or Apache women could get work doing laundry. A back alley behind the town's saloons hid brick "cribs," rows of small apartments rented by prostitutes, while basements were rumored to hide opium dens. Mexican, Croatian, Welsh, and other immigrants occupied neighborhoods of tents, shacks, and company houses. And high above on Company Row, prim Victorians housed the mine's managers and their families.

MAYBE YOU'VE RUN OUT OF things to do in Sedona. Or maybe, as some locals believe, all that red rock vortex energy has simply become too intense. Whatever the reason, expand your horizons south to tour a historic mining camp, sample some fresh-picked peaches, or hop on board a train to see a rugged canyon and maybe even a bald eagle.

You can do all of these and more in the Verde Valley, which spreads between Sedona's red cliffs and the blue slopes of Mingus Mountain in a green-and-gold quilt of grasses, creosote, and mesquite.

The valley's major waterway, the Verde River, is joined by several perennially flowing creeks. Sixteenth-century Spanish explorers first named it Rio Alamos for the cottonwoods along its banks, then Rio de los Reyes, the river of kings. The name Rio Verde, or green river, described the oasis of trees and grasses created by the river and its beaver ponds.

The settlers—like the Indians and Spanish before them—were drawn to the valley's wealth of resources: good soil, plentiful game and forage, mild climate, and valuable minerals. Today, the Verde Valley offers a wealth of scenic vistas, historic attractions, and parks and forests, with activities ranging from peaceful country drives to whitewater rafting.

Another "must-visit" community is Jerome. Nestled dramatically into the side of Mingus Mountain, the lights of Jerome twinkle enticingly above the valley each night after the sun sets. When Sedona was still an agricultural community of a few families, Jerome was a

When the mines closed in 1953, Jerome's population plummeted. But this was a town used to the vagaries of fate. Before the turn of the century, Jerome had burned down and been rebuilt three times. Fortunes rose and fell with copper prices. Even before the stock market crashed in 1929, the town began its own literal slide, creeping downhill destroying entire blocks. But after each disaster, Jerome bounced back. Young folks (hippies, some called them) moved in during the sixties and seventies, and the ghost town was reborn as an arts community.

Opposite: **This adobe mansion, now a state park, was built by James S. Douglas near his mine, better known as the Little Daisy mine.** *Above:* **A newspaperman once said Jerome's "buildings cling to the precipitous sides of the mountain. Your neighbor to the rear…can look down your chimney from his front porch."** *Pages 58-59:* **The Verde Valley is cradled between the slopes of the Black Hills and Red Rock Country.**

Jerome's steep streets and slope-hugging buildings are now home to about five hundred residents, as well as art galleries, restaurants, shops, and inns. Jerome State Historical Park preserves the adobe mansion of "Rawhide Jimmy" Douglas, with exhibits on Arizona's mining industry and the billion-dollar copper camp of Jerome.

East of Jerome, the Perkinsville Road skinnies through an old rail cut and then goes up, down, and around hills all the way north to Williams. The dirt road is a white-knuckled drive through Prescott and Kaibab National Forests, with views of the old Arizona Central rail line, Sycamore Canyon, and pine-covered Bill Williams Mountain.

Below Jerome is the postcard-pretty town of Clarkdale, built by Senator William S. Clark for a new smelter for his United Verde mine in Jerome. By 1915, the company town had modern plumbing and sewer, a town square and bandstand, and a handsome clubhouse that included a library, bowling alley, and pool. The town's charming main street looks much the same as it did in 1928, when famed lawman Jim Roberts foiled a bank robbery amidst a flurry of bullets.

Clarkdale today is headquarters for the Verde Canyon Railroad, a popular excursion train that skirts the Verde River. Riders often spot bald eagles, great blue herons, and other wildlife on the half-day trip, billed as "Arizona's longest-running nature show." The train's nearly forty-mile route cuts through a steep-walled section of Verde Canyon and edges remote Sycamore Canyon, with its colorful Redwall Limestone and Supai cliffs.

At fifty-six thousand acres, the Sycamore Canyon Wilderness Area is a haven for hikers, equestrians, and backpackers. The Parsons Trail begins at the canyon's mouth, and day-hikers will do some creek-crossing and boulder-hopping before reaching Parsons Springs, four miles up canyon. Above the springs, the creek is intermittent and the terrain rugged—backpacking requires careful planning.

Between Clarkdale and Cottonwood, a six hundred-year-old Sinaguan village perches on a hilltop overlooking the Verde River. The village was excavated in the 1930s by a pair of graduate students from the University of Arizona and a crew funded by the Civil Works Administration, part of Roosevelt's alphabet soup of economic

recovery programs. They found caches of beads and cut stone for making inlay jewelry, enormous pottery jars for storing corn, and beautifully woven cotton fabric.

Apache workers gave the national monument its name, Tuzigoot, or "crooked water." The museum's excellent collection of artifacts and displays brings to life the Sinagua's "golden age," when large hilltop towns like Tuzigoot dotted the Verde River's curving path through the valley.

Another historic landmark in the area originated in 1865, when a unit of volunteer soldiers erected a tent camp at West Clear Creek with a mission of protecting nearby farms from raids. Camp Lincoln, later renamed Fort Verde, moved to its present site on the white limestone bluffs

Above: **Lower Sycamore Canyon is lush with green in the spring, when the creek flows from snowmelt and natural springs.**

Above: Powwows hosted by the Yavapai Nation feature drum groups and dancers in elaborate regalia. *Top:* The masonry room blocks of Tuzigoot, abandoned six hundred years ago, meander across a hilltop that overlooks the cottonwood-lined Verde River.

Right: Montezuma Castle perches high above the floodplain of Beaver Creek, where Sinaguan farmers raised corn, beans, squash, and cotton.

of the Verde River in 1871. Twenty-two buildings clustered around the parade ground during the fort's heyday, making room for two cavalry companies and two companies of infantry.

Local citizens maintained the fort, which was abandoned in 1891, until it finally became Fort Verde State Historic Park in 1971. Today, visitors can tour four buildings, including the Surgeon's Quarters.

Situated at Arizona's geographical center, Camp Verde also sits between two national forests: Prescott and Coconino. The Verde Ranger Station offers information on hiking, camping, and river running. With stretches from "mild to wild," the Verde River can be a gentle family excursion or a challenging whitewater adventure. Local outfitters rent boats and lead tours during peak flows.

North of Camp Verde, the Yavapai-Apache Nation operates Cliff Castle Casino. Even if you never drop a quarter into the slots, you will still find plenty to do. The casino is also home to restaurants, a nightclub, and a bowling alley. An outdoor pavilion hosts powwows and features performances by popular rock and country bands.

Not far from this contemporary Native American community is the centuries-old cliff dwelling called Montezuma Castle, a national monument since 1906. This five-story pueblo sheltered Sinagua villagers during their last years in the Verde Valley before they abandoned their farms and homes and migrated northward.

Wet Beaver Creek flows below the ruins, creating a shady oasis of towering Arizona sycamores. The Sinagua used the trees as beams, overlying them with poles, brush, and then a thick layer of mud, so that the one room's beamed ceiling became the adobe floor of the room above. Room interiors have been closed to visitors for more than fifty years, but views of the castle are possible from the trail below.

Six miles away, Montezuma Well preserves early agricultural technology. The well is a sinkhole formed within the limestone-bearing Verde formation. Its spring-fed waters are fifty-five feet deep. (A soldier from Fort Verde checked the depth in the 1880s, floating to the middle on an air bed borrowed from the post hospital and dropping a line, dispelling rumors that it was bottomless.) The well's natural outlet, with a flow of over a million gallons a day, was diverted by prehistoric farmers to water their fields. Their canals, marked by calcium carbonate deposits from the mineral-laden water, can still be seen a thousand years later.

Between Sedona and Camp Verde lie the small communities of Cornville and Page Springs, linked by lower Oak Creek. Orchards dot the creek, and roadside produce stands sell fresh peaches, sweet corn, and other vegetables. For a taste of the old country, stop at Cornville's Manzanita Inn, especially during Oktoberfest, when the chef cooks up German specialties. Or catch your own dinner in Page Springs. A trail follows the creek opposite the fish-rearing ponds of the Page Springs fish hatchery. The hatchery is a birdwatcher's delight, drawing mergansers, warblers, flycatchers, and many other species to the creek's cottonwood-lined banks. There is a wheelchair-accessible nature trail, as well as picnic tables. The Beaverhead Flat Road makes a scenic loop back to Red Rock Country and Hwy. 179.

© 2002 by Northland Publishing
All rights reserved.

This book may not be reproduced in whole or in part, by any
means (with the exception of short quotes for the purpose of
review), without permission of the publisher. For information,
address Permissions, Northland Publishing, P. O. Box 1389,
Flagstaff, Arizona 86002-1389.

www.northlandpub.com

Composed in the United States of America
Printed in South Korea

Edited by Tammy Gales
Design and Art Direction by David Jenney
Production supervised by Donna Boyd

FIRST IMPRESSION 2002
ISBN 0-87358-818-5 (pb) / ISBN-13: 978-0-87358-818-8
ISBN 0-87358-854-1 (hc) / ISBN-13: 978-0-87358-854-6

07   06   05   6   5   4

Library of Congress Cataloging-in-Publication Data

Bryant, Kathleen.
   Sedona : treasure of the Southwest / Kathleen Bryant.
      p. cm.
   1. Sedona Region (Ariz.)—Pictorial works. 2. Sedona
Region (Ariz.)—Description and travel. 3. Sedona Region
(Ariz.)—History. 4. Natural history—Arizona—Sedona Region.
5. Oak Creek Canyon (Ariz.)—Pictorial works. 6. Oak Creek
Canyon (Ariz.)—Description and travel. 7. Oak Creek Canyon
(Ariz.)—History. 8. Natural history—Arizona—Oak Creek
Canyon. I. Title.

F819.S42 B79 2002
979.1'33—dc21   2002070160

Photography © 2002 by:

Paul Beakley: 47 (bottom)
Paul & Joyce Berquist: 3 (top right), 13, 14 (bottom left & right), 15
Dick Dietrich: 5 (top right), 30-31, 32
David Elms, Jr.: 46, 50 (top right)
George H. H. Huey: 5 (bottom right), 57 (right)
Kerrick James: 3 (top center), 10-11 (bottom spread)
Klaus Kranz: 19 (center), 61 (right)
Chuck Lawsen: iv-1, 7 (top), 18, 19 (top), 38-39 (spread), 54
Larry Lindahl: 2 (top right), 2-3 (bottom spread), 4 (bottom right) 4-5
   (top & bottom spreads), 5 (bottom left), 11 (top right), 19 (bottom), 28
   (top), 39 (top & bottom right), 40, 41, 45, 47 (top left), 61 (left)
Edward McCain: 4 (top center), 23 (top), 52-53, 60, back cover
Robert G. McDonald: ii-iii, 4 (top right), 5 (top left), 6, 8-9, 10 (top), 12,
   16-17, 20-21, 22, 23 (left), 24-25, 27 (left center), 43, 50 (bottom), 51,
   58-59, 62-63
Randy Prentice: 35 (top), 48, 50 (left), 56-57 (spread), 61 (top)
Jerry Sieve: front cover, 11 (top left), 44 (bottom)
David H. Smith: 29, 42 (top), 47 (center left), 49 (bottom), 55
Tom Till: 26
Larry Ulrich: 7 (bottom), 14-15 (top spread), 44 (top), 49 (top)

Pages 2 (bottom center), 3 (bottom left), 4 (bottom left), 33, 34, 35
   (bottom left & right), 36: Courtesy of Sedona Historical Society
Pages 3 (top left), 37 (top left & bottom): Courtesy of Photofest
Page 37 (top right): Courtesy of Richard & Sherry Mangum
Page 42 (bottom): Courtesy of Garland's Navajo Rugs
Page 47 (right center): Courtesy of Sedona Golf Resort

All Rights Reserved.